101 CHRISTMAS JOKES

THE HENNESSY KIDS

THE HENNESSY ENTERTAINMENT COMPANY

101 Christmas Jokes / by The Hennessy Kids

ISBN 978-1-9994854-2-9 (Print)

ISBN 978-1-9994854-3-6 (E-book)

1. Christmas - Juvenile humour. 2. Wit and humor, Juvenile. I. The Hennessy Kids, author.

The Hennessy Entertainment Company | HennessyEnt.com |

Copyright © 2022 by The Hennessy Entertainment Company

All rights reserved.

No part of this book may be reproduced in any form or by any electronic or mechanical means, including information storage and retrieval systems, without written permission from the author, except for the use of brief quotations in a book review.

 Created with Vellum

For Grammie & Grampie and Nana & Papa. Love you!

1
CHRISTMAS FOOD

What is a snowman's favourite breakfast?
    Frosted Flakes.

What never eats at Christmas?
    The turkey - it's stuffed.

What is the crankiest winter food?
    A brrrrr-grrrrr.

What does a snowman call a block of snow?
    An ice crispie square.

Why did the turkey cross the road?
    Because he wasn't chicken.

What do snowmen eat for lunch at the North Pole?
    Icebergers.

Elves make sandwiches with what kind of bread?
    Shortbread.

What's the best thing to put into a Christmas cookie?
    Your teeth.

What did the gingerbread man put under his blankets?
    A cookie sheet.

How do salt, pepper, nutmeg, cinnamon, and mint sign their Christmas cards?
    Seasons greetings.

Why was the turkey asked to join the North Pole Band?
    Because he had the drum sticks.

2
ALL ABOUT SANTA

Who says "Oh! Oh! Oh!"
    Santa walking backwards.

Who delivers presents to baby sharks at Christmas?
    Santa Jaws.

Why did Santa put a clock in his sleigh?
    He wanted to see time fly.

What happens to Santa get if he's stuck in a chimney?
    He gets claustrophobic.

Why does Santa have three gardens?
    So he can ho, ho, ho.

What is the name of Santa's dog?
　　Santa Paws.

Where does Santa stay on vacation?
　　At the ho-ho-hotel.

How do you know Santa is good at jiu-jitsu?
　　Because he has a black belt.

How much did Santa pay for his sleigh?
　　Nothing - it was on the house.

How did Santa Claus open the front door?
　　He used a tur-key

What does Santa use in his washing machine?
　　Yule-Tide.

What do the elves call it when their boss claps his hands?
　　Santapplause.

What do you call a creature that's half-horse, half-Santa?
　　A santaur.

What do they use at the North Pole to kill germs?
 Santa-tizer.

3
SANTA'S HELPERS

What happens to elves when they behave naughty?
    Santa gives them the sack.

What kind of music do elves listen to?
    Wrap.

What can you say about a greedy elf?
    He's elfish.

What's the first thing Santa's helpers learn at school?
    The elfabet.

What kind of cars do elves drive?
    Toy-otas.

What do you call an elf who steals gift wrapping paper from the rich and gives it to the poor?
Ribbon Hood

What units of measurement do elves use in the workshop?
Santameters.

How do the elves capture memories at the workshop?
They take elfies using North Pole-aroids.

The elves use use solar and wind power in the workshop.
You could say it's elf-sufficient.

Why did the elf push his bed into the fireplace?
He wanted to sleep like a log.

Eleven elves already in the workshop. What do you call the next elf to join?
The twelf.

How do elves get to the top floor of Santa's workshop?
    They use the elf-evator.

What do the elves cook with in the kitchen?
    Utinsel.

How does an elf get to Santa's workshop?
    By icicle.

4

THE REINDEER

Which of Santa's reindeer has bad manners?
   Rude-olph.

Did you know Rudolph never went to school?
   He was elf-taught.

Why did Santa only have eight reindeer?
   Comet stayed home to clean the sink.

What's the difference between Santa's reindeer and a knight?
   One is dragging the sleigh, the other is slaying the dragon.

What does a reindeer say before telling you a joke?
   This one is going to sleigh you.

How does Rudolph know when Christmas is coming?
    He refers to his calen-deer.

If a reindeer lost his tail, where would it go for a new one?
    A re-tail shop.

Which reindeer have the shortest legs?
    The smallest ones.

How do you make a slow reindeer fast?
    You don't feed it.

What do reindeer have that no other animals have?
    Baby reindeer.

Which reindeer should you ask to the snow ball?
    Dancer.

What do reindeer use when they go fishing?
    Their ant-lures.

How do you get into Rudolph's house?
    You ring the deer-bell.

THE HENNESSY KIDS

Where do the reindeer like to stop for lunch?
    Deery Queen.

How do reindeers sign cards to their cousins?
    Merry Christmoose!

5
A STOCKING FULL OF JOKES

What has a jolly laugh, brings your presents and scratches up your furniture?
    Santa Claws.

What do reindeer hang on their Christmas trees?
    Horn-aments.

Knock knock!
    Who's there?
    Holly
    Holly who?
    Holly-days are here again.

Why did Scrooge keep a pet lamb?
    Because it would say, "Baaaaahh humbug!"

Why is it always cold at Christmas?
Because it's in Decembrrrrr.

What can you get if you eat Christmas decorations?
Tinselitus.

What do you get when you cross an apple with a Christmas tree?
A pineapple

What do you get when Santa Claus investigates missing toys?
Santa Clues.

Knock-knock.
Who's there?
Olive.
Olive who?
Olive the other reindeer.

What did the cow say on Christmas morning?
Mooooey Christmas

What happens if your rocket stalls on Christmas Eve?
You get a mistletoe.

Knock-knock.
> Who's there?
> Mary.
> Mary who?
> Mary Christmas.

When is a boat just like snow?
> When its adrift.

Knock-knock.
> Who's there?
> Snow.
> Snow who?
> Snow use - I've forgotten my name.

What does December have that no other month has?
> The letter D.

What type of pine has the sharpest needles?
> A porcupine.

What do you call a chicken at the North Pole?
> Lost.

How do cats greet each other at Christmas?
> Have a Furry Merry Christmas and a Happy Mew Year!

What is a skunk's favourite song?
Jingle Smells.

What is a librarian's favourite song for library nights?
Silent Night.

What dog is mentioned in Jingle Bells?
Daschund through the snow.

What is whip cream's favourite Christmas song?
"We Whisk You A Merry Christmas."

Knock-knock.
Who's there?
Hannah.
Hannah who.
Hannah a partridge in a pear tree.

Knock-knock.
Who's there?
Murray.
Murray who?
Murray Christmas.

Knock-knock.
> Who's there?
> Pizza.
> Pizza who?
> Pizza on earth and good will toward men.

Knock-knock.
> Who's there.
> Dexter.
> Dexter who?
> Dexter halls with boughs of holly.

6

DECORATIONS

Why are Christmas trees so bad at sewing?
    They always drop their needles.

What happened to the thief who stole an Advent calendar?
    He got twenty-five days.

What do you call a frog hanging from the ceiling?
    Mistletoad.

Where do mistletoe go to become famous?
    Holly wood.

Who is a Christmas tree's favourite singer?
    Spruce Springsteen.

7
PRESENTS

What's the best Christmas present?
    You can't beat a broken drum.

Why is Darth Vader tough to surprise on Christmas?
    Because he can sense your presents.

I asked for a Star Wars car.
    They gave me a toy Yoda.

One Christmas I got a pack of batteries with a note saying, "Toy not included."

How many presents can Santa fit in an empty sack?
    Only one – after that it's not empty any more.

8
SNOWPEOPLE

Why was the snowman rooting in the bag of carrots?
　He was picking his nose.

What do you call Frosty the Snowman in summer?
　A puddle.

Where does Frosty keep his money?
　In the snow bank.

Why does everybody like Frosty the Snowman?
　Because he is cool.

What does Frosty like the most about school?
　Snow and tell.

What does Frosty think about?
Snow idea.

Where does Frosty and his girlfriend go to dance?
The snowball.

How do you know that a snowman is not in a good mood?
When he gives you the cold shoulder.

What's a snowman's favourite Mexican food?
Brrrrrr-itos.

What song do you sing at a snowman's birthday party?
Freeze a jolly good fellow!

Who helps you lift your car when you get a flat tire during winter?
Jack Frost.

WORD SEARCH

```
I D V S R F W I N T E R T H G
S Z D R H A Q N S N O W O U I
O C I U A M N W Q K I J Y G V
C S Y D P I T I H H A H X H E
K L Z O P L T S O R N T M Y P
S E V L Y Y O H L G A M E N C
K D Y P D V Y X I P H Z U A V
I R E H M C S R D F R O S T Y
F P E S P S O G A E Y L V H M
R T R I E T S O Y L M E R R Y
I K I E N R R L K F V T T T W
E C W N S D T E E I J T R B G
N M V R S E E K A D E E E O G
D A K E A E N E T T P R E W V
S A T T X P L T R Y C H E E R
```

BOW	HOLIDAY	SNOW
CHEER	HUG	SOCK
COOKIE	LETTER	TINSEL
ELF	MERRY	TOY
FAMILY	PRESENT	TOYS
FRIENDS	REINDEER	TREAT
FROSTY	RUDOLPH	TREE
GAME	SKATE	WINTER
GIVE	SKI	WISH
HAPPY	SLED	WRAP

10

YOUR FAVOURITE JOKE

What is your favourite Christmas joke that isn't in this book?

Send it to us at thehennessykids@gmail.com, and we'll look to share it online with all our friends!

Merry Christmas!

Thank you for reading our book! We hope you enjoyed it.
Please tell these jokes to your friends and family and make more people happy.

ABOUT THE AUTHORS

The Hennessy Kids think the world would be better with more smiles.

Want to know when our new books are available? Sign up for our **Fun Stuff With Heart** newsletter at HennessyEnt.com!

BOOKS BY THE HENNESSY KIDS

101 Halloween Jokes

101 Christmas Jokes

101 Pet Jokes

101 Knock Knock Jokes, Vol. 1

101 Nature Jokes

101 Food Jokes

www.ingramcontent.com/pod-product-compliance
Lightning Source LLC
Chambersburg PA
CBHW052127070526
44586CB00016B/2115